RAISING A FOREST

THIBAUD HEREM

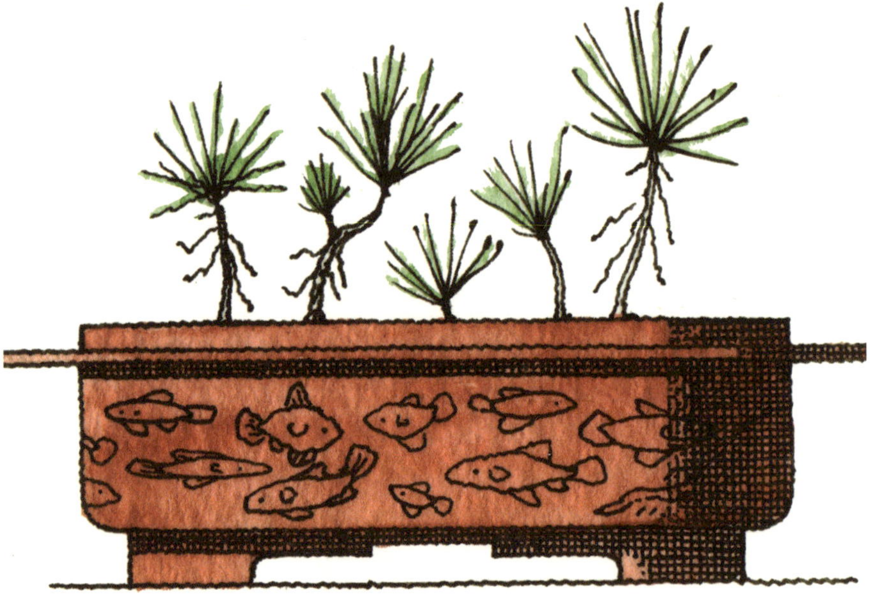

CONTENTS

	PAGES
INTRO	4-5
MY BENCH IN WINTER	6-7
SEEDS	8-9
PHILOSOPHY	10-11
JAPANESE BLACK PINE / SILVER BIRCH	12-13
CHERRY TREE / SCOTS PINE	14-15
CEDARS	16-17
REDWOODS	18-19
MAPLES	20-21
TOOLS	22-23
MY BENCH IN SPRING	24-25
YEW / OLIVE TREE	26-27
STONE PINE / HAWTHORN	28-29
POTS	30-31
OAKS	32-33
MY BENCH IN SUMMER	34-35
HINOKI / GINKGO	36-37
PRUNUS / LARCH	38-39
COTONEASTER / PINUS STROBUS	40-41
MY BENCH IN AUTUMN	42-43

3

FOLIAGE CROWN APEX

TRUNK BRANCH TWIG

ROOT HAIR ZONE

TAP ROOT

INTRO

Five years ago my flatmate came back from work with two packets of seeds given to him by one of his clients. Out of a lazy curiosity, I planted the seeds in a yogurt tub in our kitchen. Two weeks later a tiny green pine needle emerged, and I was taken aback by the sense of pride I felt towards the little sprout.

I come from a long line of farmers in Brittany, France. From the age of 14, I spent summers working on my grandparents' and uncle's farms, tending to their vegetables, in tune with fluctuations of weather and natural environment. But that seems like ancient history now. I moved to London 12 years ago, and gradually grew blind to the variations of grey weather and pollution. The adrenaline and energy of a city is a pleasure that supersedes all that. Like a lot of people, I mostly ignore the nagging guilt at being complicit in a system of relentless consumerism that does so much damage to the planet.

Despite not having a balcony or any outside space, those tiny seeds had managed to grow roots and emerge into the light. I felt the magic of being part of something bigger, and a sense of awe at the immense power of nature. It made me feel hopeful. Since then I have moved into a flat with a garden. It's small, but it's something. Gradually I have filled my garden with fifty species of trees. They are mostly grown from seeds, and I often imagine them fully grown, their roots deep in the earth, their branches reaching to the sun, thick with foliage. I think of them standing for fifty, a hundred, two hundred years.

This is the story of my obsession with trees and the process of growing them.

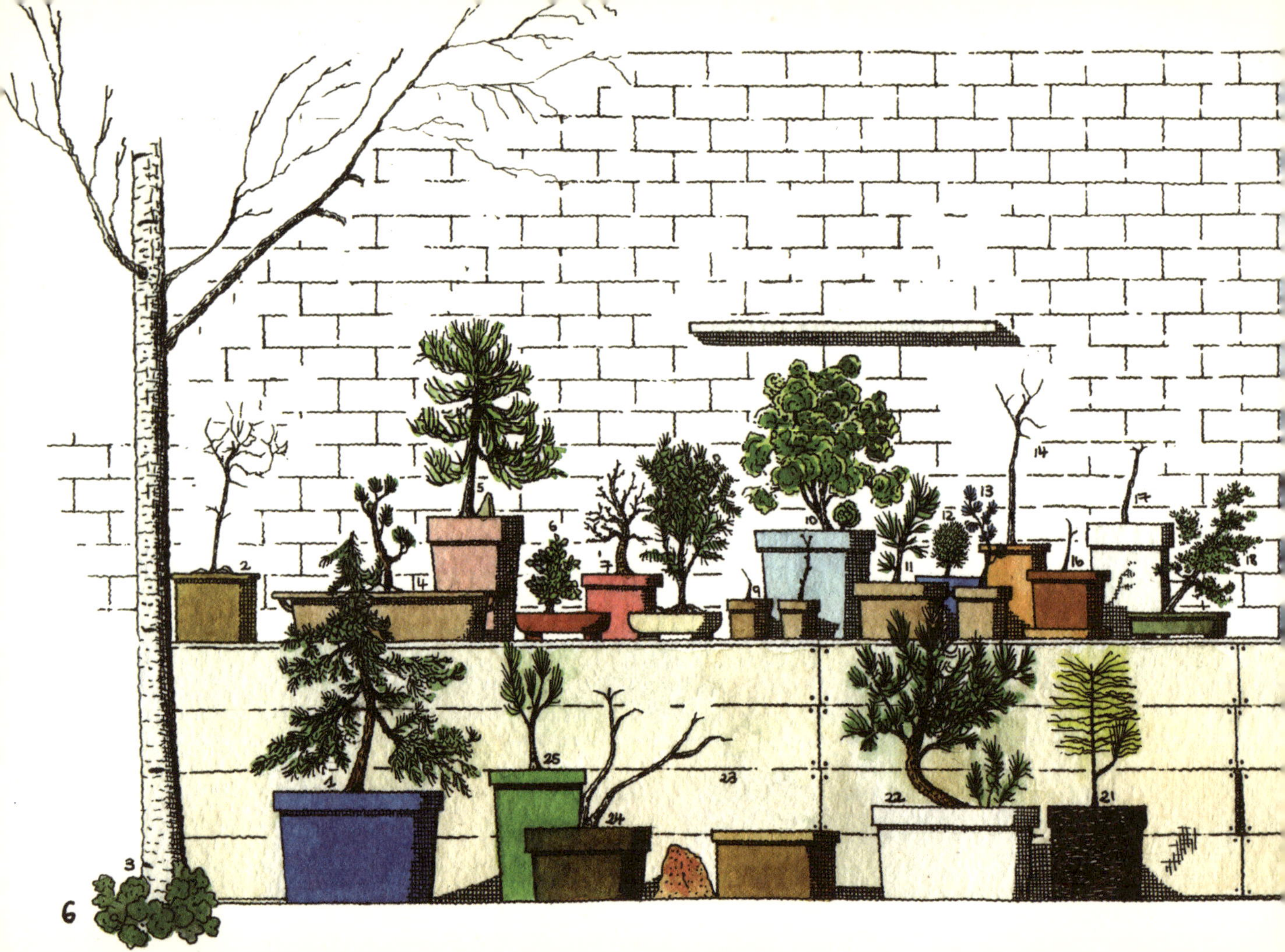
1
2
3
4
5
6
7
8
9
10
11
12
13
14
16
17
18
21
22
23
24
25

MY BENCH IN WINTER.

Trees are dormant in winter, and therefore trauma resistant, so it's a good time to prepare your garden for spring.

You can repot and clean your trees without causing any damage, so that when they wake up again in spring they'll quickly adapt to their new environment.

1. COASTAL REDWOOD
2. GINKGO
3. SILVER BIRCH
4. JAPANESE WHITE PINE
5. GIANT SEQUOIA
6. COTONEASTER CORAL BEAUTY
7. LARCH
8. YEW
9. OAK
10. HINOKI CYPRESS
11. SCOTS PINE
12. PINUS STROBUS
13. ATLAS CEDAR
14. OLIVE TREE
15. SUCCULENTS
16. TRIDENT MAPLE
17. MOUNTAIN MAPLE
18. SAN JOSE JUNIPER
19. COLORADO BLUE SPRUCE
20. PRUNUS DOMESTICA
21. JAPANESE RED PINE
22. JAPANESE BLACK PINE
23. BOXWOOD
24. FIGTREE
25. STONE PINE

SEEDS

I love walking in the woods in autumn, looking at the trees around me and foraging for their seeds on the ground. I look for closed cones, which I then dry out at home, carefully shaking out their seeds when they open up and storing them in bags, until I am ready to plant in late winter. I aim for the seeds to germinate in early spring, so that the weather is clement when stored outside.

- I start by planting the seeds in a mini-greenhouse — which is effectively a tray with holes in it and a clear plastic top.

IF COLLECTING SEEDS IN NATURE IS DIFFICULT OR YOU WANT TO BE MORE ADVENTUROUS WITH YOUR CHOICE OF SPECIMENS, YOU CAN PICK UP SEEDS FOR PRETTY MUCH ANY SPECIES ONLINE, OR BUY SMALL TREES FROM NURSERIES. BUT THERE IS A MAGIC TO GROWING TREES FROM SEEDS THAT I WOULD HIGHLY RECOMMEND.

WHEN THEY OUTGROW THE MINI-GREENHOUSE, I REPOT THEM IN SMALL INDIVIDUAL POTS.

SHOOTS EMERGE AFTER A FEW WEEKS (TO A COUPLE OF MONTHS).

THE PRIMARY LEAVES FALL OFF AND SECONDARY LEAVES BEGIN TO GROW IN.

WHEN THE SECONDARY LEAVES ARE ESTABLISHED, I MOVE THE SEEDLINGS OUTSIDE.

PHILOSOPHY:

A touchstone on my journey has been "The Man Who Planted Trees" by Jean Giono.
It's a fictional tale of a young man who comes across a dry, deserted wasteland in the foothills of the Alps. The sole inhabitant is a shepherd, who, as he walks the land, plants acorns harvested from many miles away.

The young man fights in World War I and returns to the valley 20 years later to find a verdant forest, rich with wildlife, and a community of people who have chosen to live in this beautiful Garden of Eden. It's a gorgeously written, hopeful tale about the power of nature to heal itself and others and about the power of humans to restore as well as destroy.

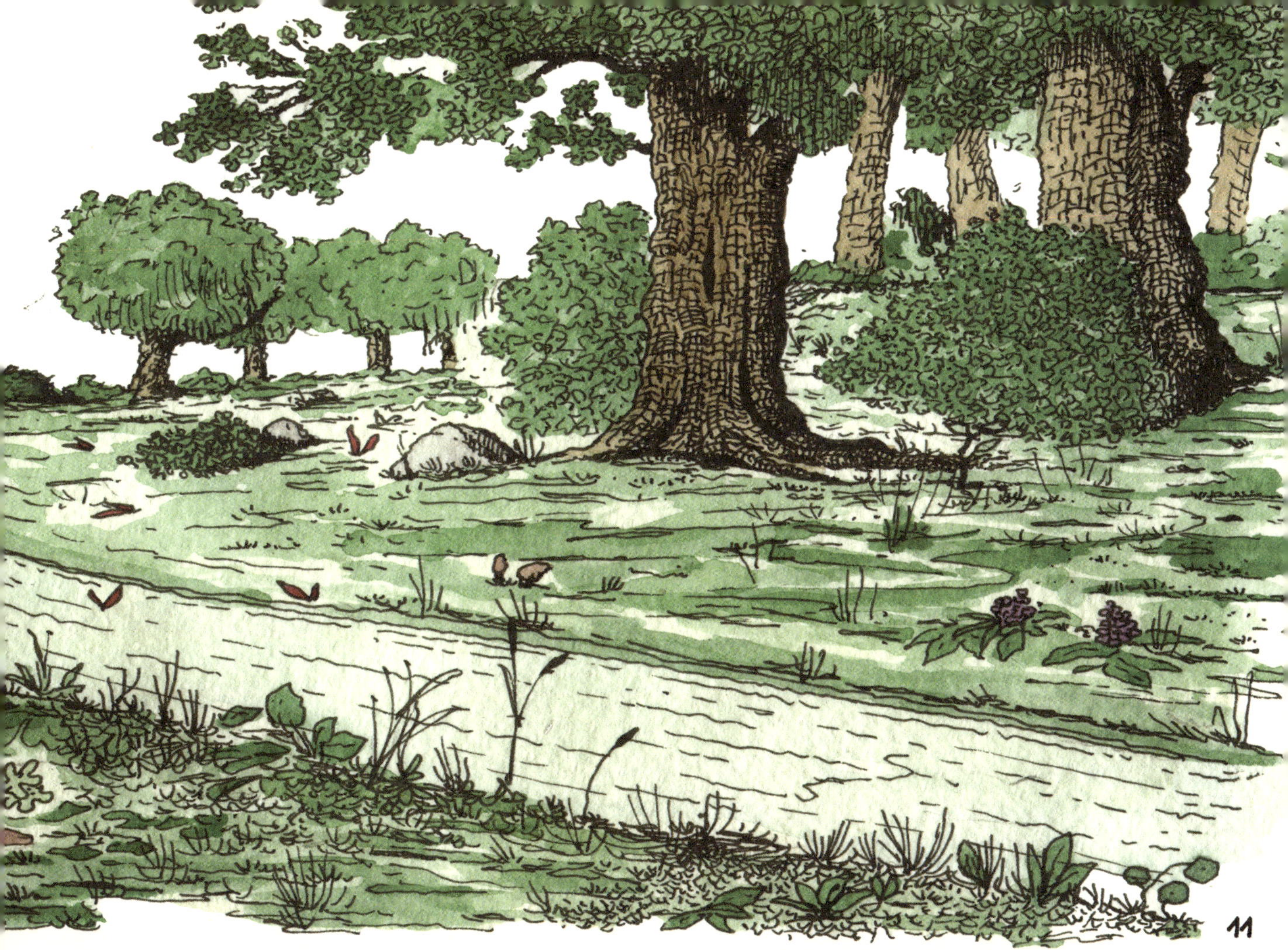

JAPANESE BLACK PINE.

PINUS THUNBERGII
FAM. PINACEAE

DIRECT SUNLIGHT.

NATIVE TO COASTAL REGIONS OF JAPAN AND KOREA. THE FOLIAGE IS EASILY COAXED INTO ELEGANT SHAPES, WHICH IS WHY IT IS A COMMON TREE FOR BONSAI ENTHUSIASTS.

EMERGING SEEDLINGS PREFER INDIRECT SUNLIGHT.

EXTREMELY POLLUTION RESISTANT, THIS IS A GOOD CHOICE FOR A CITY GARDENER.

WHEN 20 CM HIGH, YOU CAN PLANT IN PROPER SOIL IN DIRECT SUNLIGHT.

BARK IS GREY ON YOUNG TREES, TURNING TO BLACK AS THE TREE MATURES.

SILVER BIRCH.
BETULA PENDULA
FAM: BETULACEAE

TOLERANT OF A RANGE OF TEMPERATURES — IT'S EQUALLY COMFORTABLE IN LONDON AND IN SPAIN.

FLYING SEEDS.

SMALL, PALE TRIANGULAR LEAVES CREATE A LIGHT CANOPY FROM ELEGANTLY DROOPY BRANCHES.

MY BIRCH IS ONE OF THE FEW TREES I BOUGHT AS A SMALL TREE. IT'S A FAST GROWER AND IN THE YEAR THAT I'VE HAD IT, THE TRUNK HAS DOUBLED IN CIRCUMFERENCE.

BARK IS WHITE YEAR ROUND. IF YOU STROKE THE BARK IN AUTUMN, THE TREE WILL SHED ITS 'EXTRA SKIN' BECOMING EVEN WHITER.

DEEP ROOTS ALLOW SURROUNDING PLANTLIFE TO THRIVE WITHOUT DRAINING NUTRIENTS.

CHERRY TREE.

PRUNUS AVIUM
FAM. ROSACEAE.

ONCE THE SEEDLING REACHES 20 CM, PLANT IN PERMANENT LOCATION.

KEEP THE SEEDS MOIST IN THE FRIDGE FOR 90 DAYS.

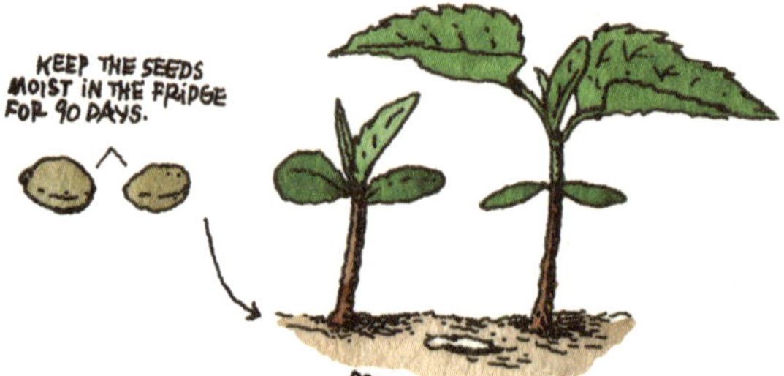

PROTECT THE SEEDLINGS FROM THE FROST

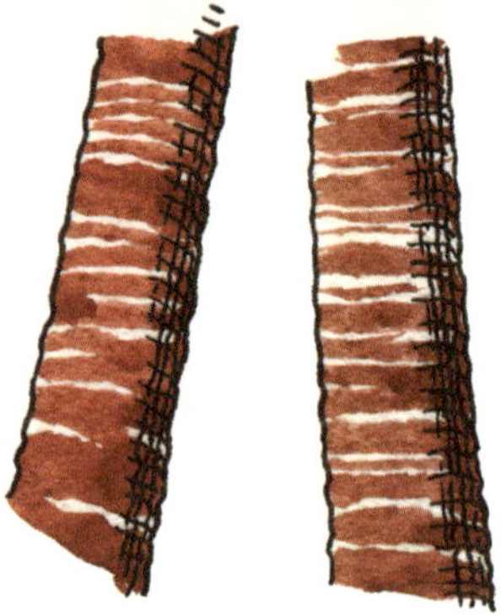

A DEEP RED BARK WITH WHITE, HORIZONTAL MARKINGS.

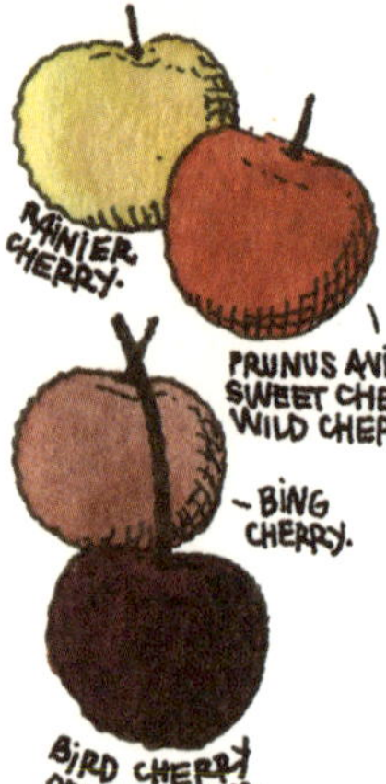

RAINIER CHERRY.

PRUNUS AVIUM: SWEET CHERRY WILD CHERRY.

BING CHERRY.

BIRD CHERRY PRUNUS PADUS.

THE FIVE-PETALLED FLOWERS HANG IN CLUSTERS.

CHERRY BLOSSOM IS KNOWN AS SAKURA IN JAPAN.

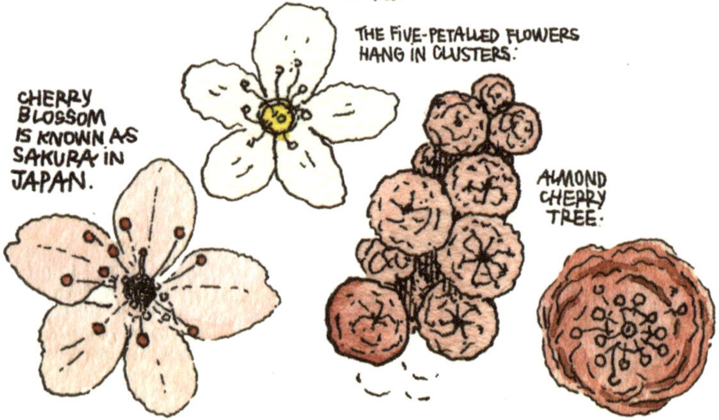

ALMOND CHERRY TREE.

THERE ARE DIFFERENT VARIETIES OF CHERRY TREE.
I HAVE A WILD CHERRY TREE AND AN ALMOND CHERRY TREE, WHICH PRODUCE MAGNIFICIENT BLOSSOM IN SPRING.

THE FRUITS VARY WITH THE VARIETY OF TREE AND ARE USUALLY FAVOURITES OF BIRDS, WHO THEN DISPERSE THE SEEDS.

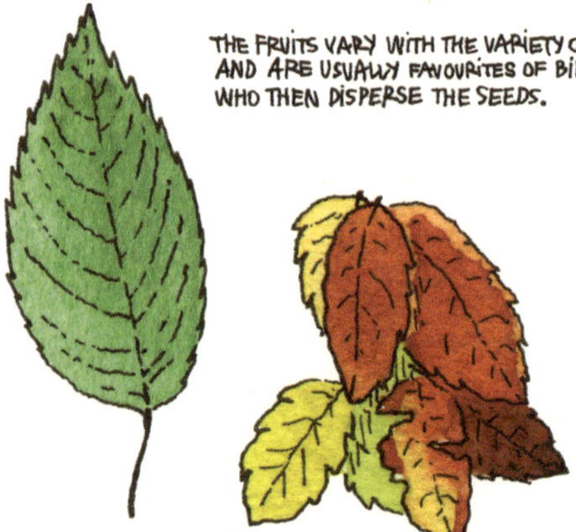

OVAL, TOOTHED LEAVES THAT HAVE MARVELLOUS AUTUMN COLOURS.

SCOTS PINE.
PINUS SYLVESTRIS
FAM. PINACEAE.

4 TO 7 CM.

THIS IS A COMMON TREE IN BRITAIN WITH A LOVELY ORANGEY-GREY BARK. IT IS ONE OF MY FAVOURITE MATURE TREES THAT I SPOT EVERYWHERE.

2 CM WINGS.

THIS WAS ONE OF THE FIRST SEEDS THAT I HARVESTED FROM CONES.

PAIRED, MEDIUM SIZE NEEDLES - 3 TO 5 CM.

PUT INTO THE GROUND ONCE THE SEEDLING REACHES 20 CM.

15

CEDARS.
CEDRUS
FAM: PINACEAE

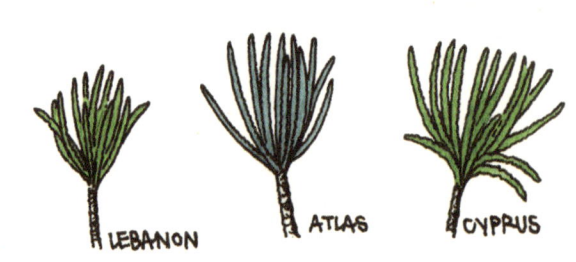

PLANT DIRECTLY IN TRAY IN SPRING.

DEODAR • LEBANON • ATLAS • CYPRUS

THERE ARE FIVE VARIETY OF CEDARS, ALL QUITE SIMILAR. I HAVE AN ATLAS CEDAR, WHICH ORIGINATES IN MOROCCO. IT HAS SMALL, ROUNDED CONES AND A STUNNING ICY-BLUE COLOUR.

MATURE TREES ARE RECEPTIVE TO LICHEN

THEY HAVE A THICK, RIDGED BARK AND EVERGREEN NEEDLE-LIKE LEAVES THAT GROW IN SPIRAL CLUSTERS ON SHORT SHOOTS.

SEED CONES ARE SIMILAR TO THOSE OF FIR TREES. THEY START OUT GREEN AND TURN BROWN, AND AT MATURITY THEY DISINTEGRATE TO RELEASE WINGED SEEDS.

Cedrus Atlantica 'Glauca Pendula'

The Weeping Blue Atlas Cedar

The shape of cedars is broad and graceful with a wide canopy branching off a relatively slim trunk.

They look a bit like fir trees, but are not direct relatives.

Native to the mountains of the Himalayas and the Mediterranean, cedars are coniferous trees that can grow up to 60m tall.

Lebanon Cedar

REDWOODS
SEQUOIOIDEAE
FAM: CUPRESSACEAE

DAWN REDWOOD.
METASEQUOIA
FAM. CUPRESSACEAE

VERY SMALL SEEDS COMPARED TO THE SIZE OF A MATURE TREE.

GIANT SEQUOIA.
SEQUOIADENDRON GIGANTEUM
FAM. CUPRESSACEAE
ENDANGERED

4 TO 4 CM.

THERE ARE THREE SPECIES OF REDWOOD, ONLY ONE OF THEM IS DECIDUOUS: THE DAWN REDWOOD.

I SOWED MY SEQUOIA 5 YEARS AGO. AFTER 3 MONTHS, THE SEEDLING WAS ALREADY 10 CM HIGH. TODAY IT IS NEARLY AS HIGH AS ME.

SPRING   SUMMER   AUTUMN

UPRIGHT. RED BEAUTIFUL BARK.

COASTAL REDWOOD.

SEQUOIA SUPERVIRENS
FAM. CUPRESSACEAE
ENDANGERED

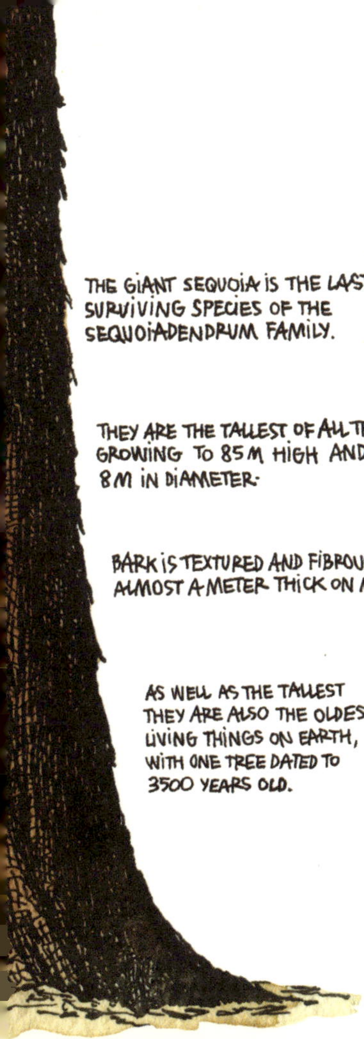

SMALLER CONES - ONLY 2-3 CM.

IT GROWS IN THE FOGGY COASTAL AREAS OF NORTHERN CALIFORNIA AND LIKES A LOT OF WATER.

THE GIANT SEQUOIA IS THE LAST SURVIVING SPECIES OF THE SEQUOIADENDRUM FAMILY.

BIGGER, FLATTER LEAVES THAN THE GIANT SEQUOIA.

THEY ARE THE TALLEST OF ALL TREES, GROWING TO 85M HIGH AND 8M IN DIAMETER.

BARK IS TEXTURED AND FIBROUS, AND CAN BE ALMOST A METER THICK ON MATURE TREES.

EACH FLOOR HAS 3 BRANCHES COMING OUT OF THE TRUNK.

AS WELL AS THE TALLEST THEY ARE ALSO THE OLDEST LIVING THINGS ON EARTH, WITH ONE TREE DATED TO 3500 YEARS OLD.

NEW BUDS CALLED "SUCKERS" GROW BETWEEN EACH FLOOR AND SHOULD BE PRUNED.

THE LARGEST OF ALL THE TREES.

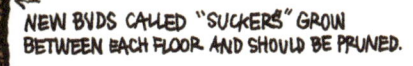

EVERY YEAR THE TREE GROWS TWO "FLOORS".

JAPANESE MAPLES.
ACER PALMATUM
FAM. SAPINDACEAE

THE SEEDS ARE ENCASED IN A FRUIT CALLED A "SEMARA".

THE "GIANT MOON" VARIETY HAS BIGGER, GREEN LEAVES WITH A PINK TINGE AND LESS SEASONAL COLOUR CHANGE.

JAPANESE MAPLES ARE SMALL, GRACEFUL DECIDUOUS TREES WITH DELICATE FOLIAGE.

PRIMARY LEAF

THEY LIKE PARTIAL SHADE AND WELL-DRAINED SOIL.

MOUNTAIN MAPLES HAVE DEEPLY DISSECTED LEAVES.

I HAVE A TRIDENT VARIETY OF JAPANESE MAPLE, WHICH HAS SIMPLER LEAVES, BUT BRILLIANT AUTUMN FOLIAGE. IT IS ONE OF MY FAVOURITES TREES IN MY COLLECTION.

IN WINTER, WHEN THE LEAVES HAVE SHED, THE DELICATE BRANCH STRUCTURE BECOMES APPARENT.

THE JAPANESE MAPLE IS A DISTANT RELATIVE OF THE GIANT CANADIAN MAPLE,

BUT THEY LIKE THE SAME, SLIGHTLY ACIDIC SOIL WITH PLENTY OF ORGANIC MATTER.

21

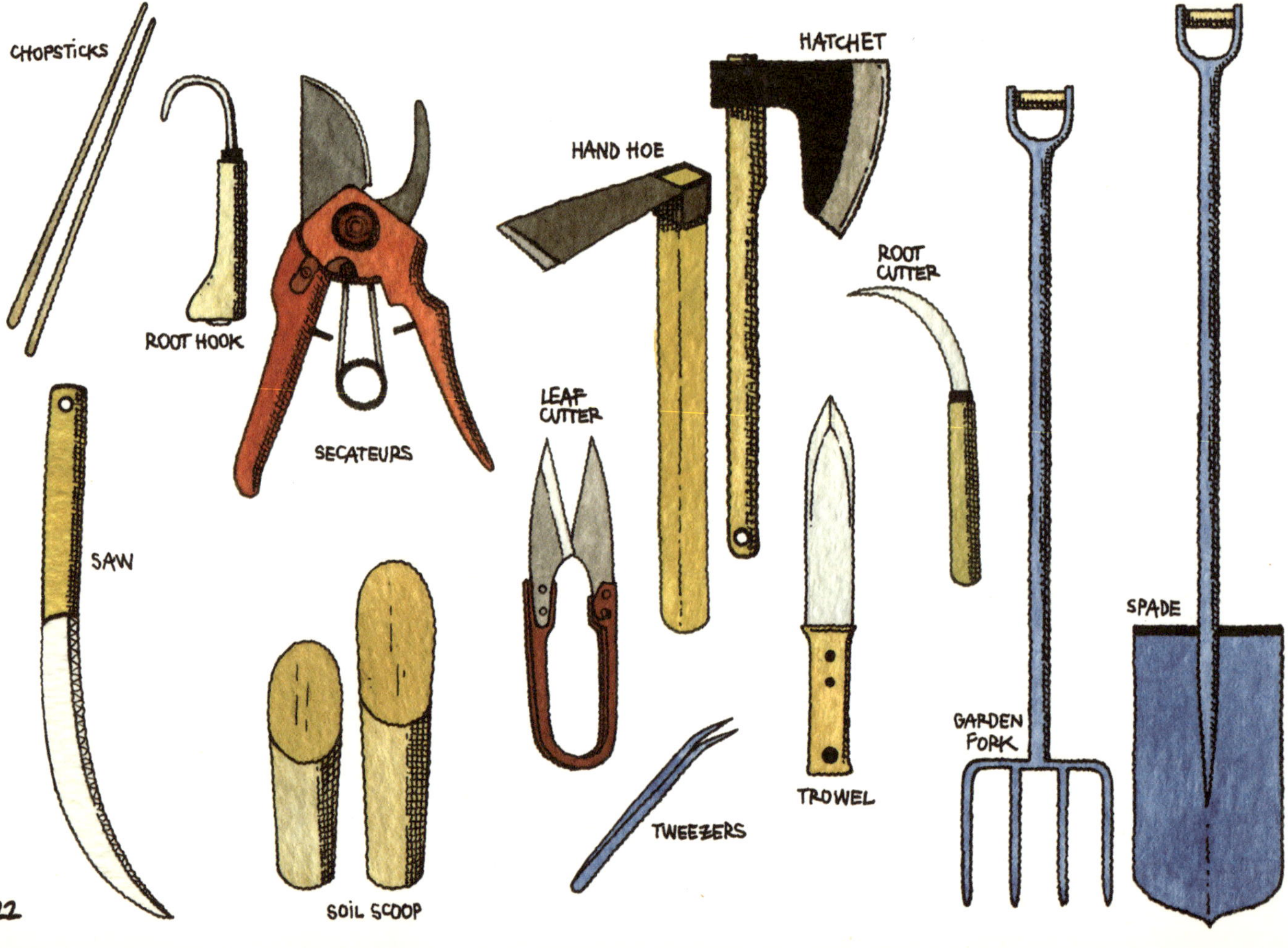
CHOPSTICKS
ROOT HOOK
SECATEURS
HAND HOE
HATCHET
ROOT CUTTER
LEAF CUTTER
SAW
SOIL SCOOP
TWEEZERS
TROWEL
GARDEN FORK
SPADE

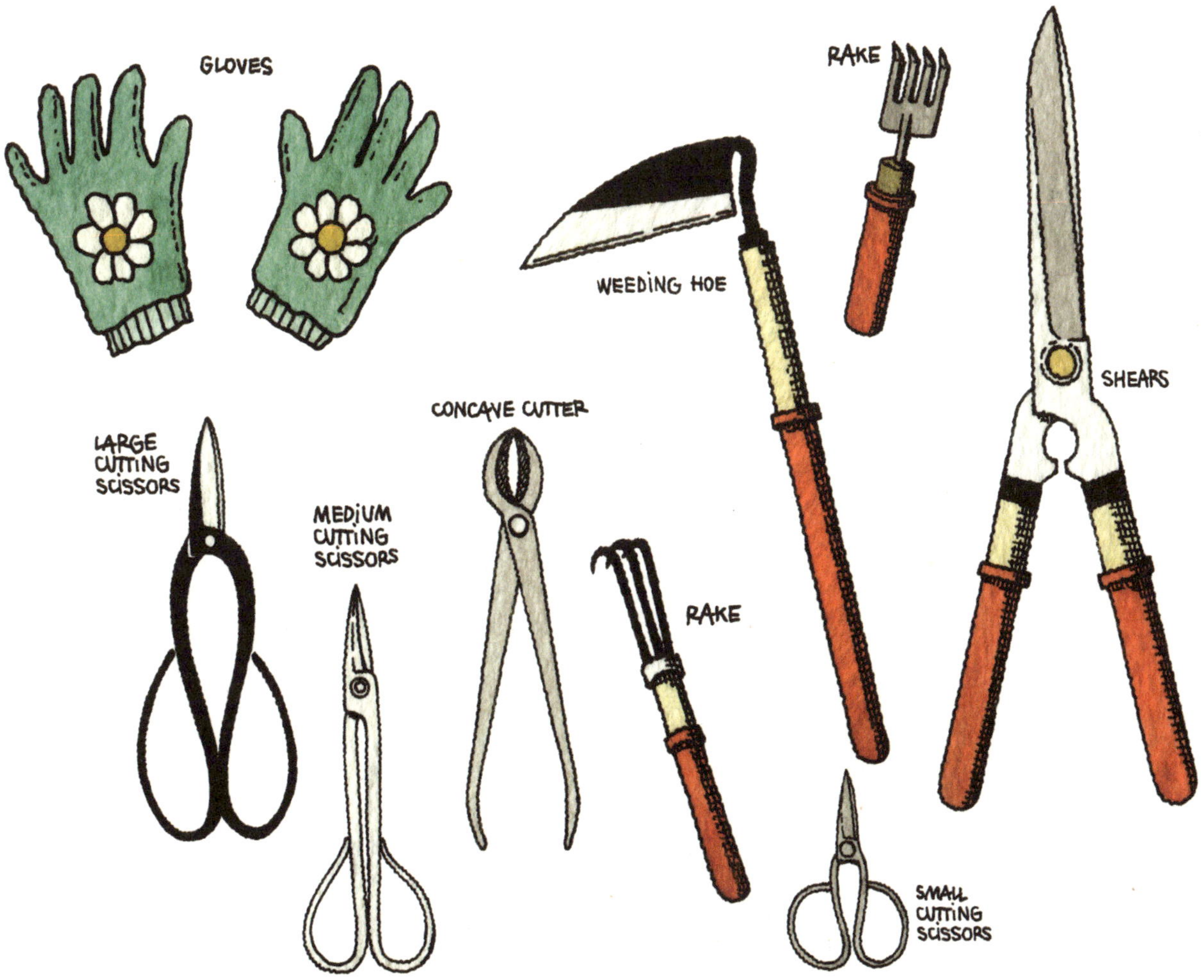
GLOVES
RAKE
WEEDING HOE
SHEARS
CONCAVE CUTTER
LARGE CUTTING SCISSORS
MEDIUM CUTTING SCISSORS
RAKE
SMALL CUTTING SCISSORS

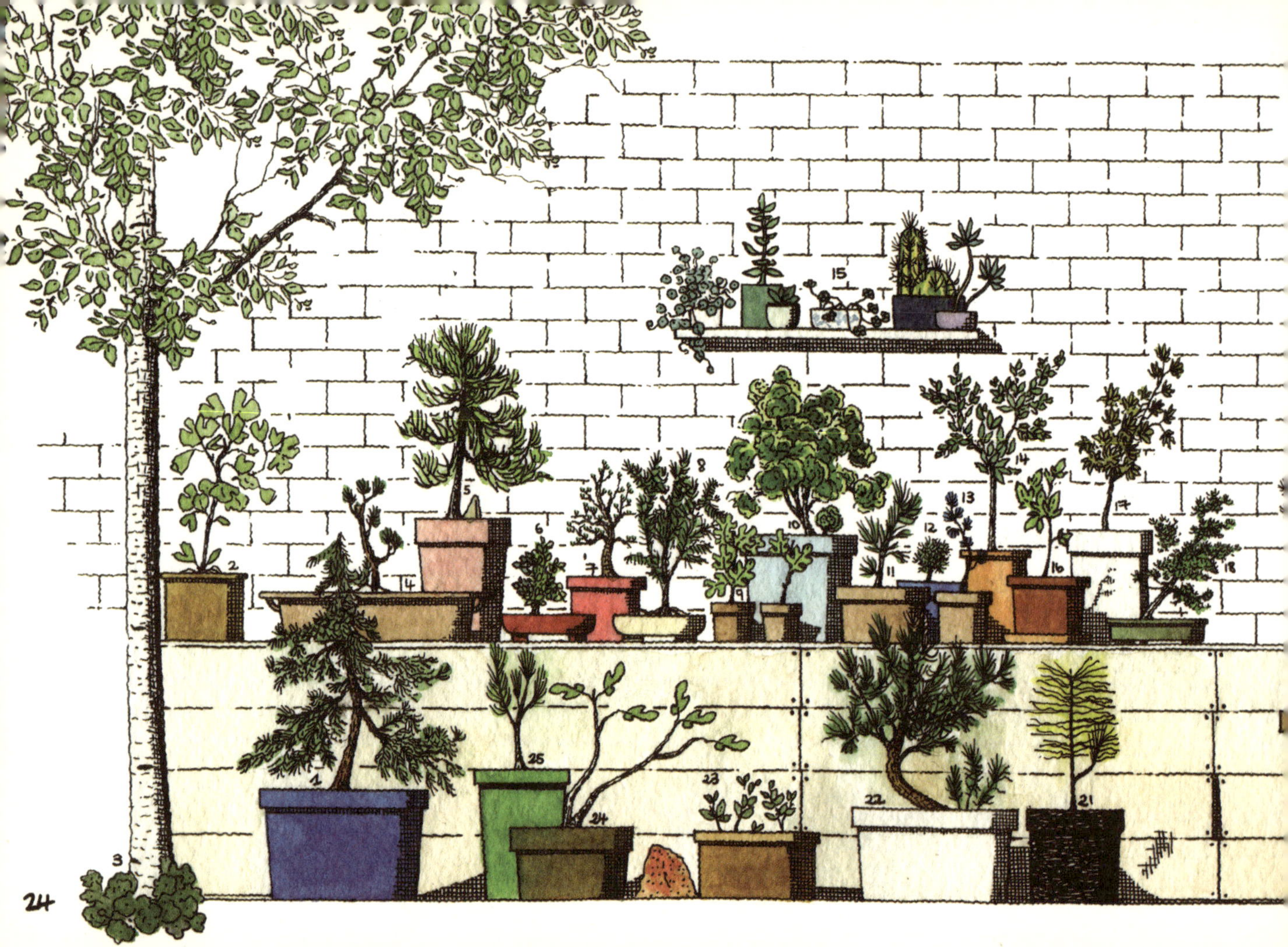
1
2
3
4
5
6
7
8
9
10
11
12
13
14
15
16
17
18
21
22
23
24
25

MY BENCH IN SPRING

SPRING IS THE MOST MAGICAL SEASON — THE DECIDUOUS TREES UNFURL THEIR LEAVES, THE FAST GROWERS SHOOT UP AND COLOURS RETURN TO MY WORKBENCH, FILLING ME WITH HOPE AND ANTICIPATION.
SPRING IS THE TIME FOR REPOTTING AND FOR PRUNING ROOTS, MAKING THE MOST OF THE TREES' INVIGORATED STATE TO ENSURE THEIR OPTIMUM HEALTH.

1. COASTAL REDWOOD
2. GINKGO
3. SILVER BIRCH
4. JAPANESE WHITE PINE
5. GIANT SEQUOIA
6. COTONEASTER CORAL BEAUTY
7. LARCH
8. YEW
9. OAK
10. HINOKI CYPRESS
11. SCOTS PINE
12. PINUS STROBUS
13. ATLAS CEDAR

14. OLIVE TREE
15. SUCCULENTS
16. TRIDENT MAPLE
17. MOUNTAIN MAPLE
18. SAN JOSE JUNIPER
19. COLORADO BLUE SPRUCE
20. PRUNUS DOMESTICA
21. JAPANESE RED PINE
22. JAPANESE BLACK PINE
23. BOXWOOD
24. FIGTREE
25. STONE PINE

ENGLISH YEW.
TAXUS BACCATA
FAM. TAXACEAE

PURPLE-RED BARK.

SMALL, STRAIGHT NEEDLES THAT GROW IN ROWS ON EITHER SIDE OF THE TWIG.

RATHER THAN CONES, YEW SEEDS GROW IN RED BERRIES.

IN ANCIENT TIMES THE TREE SYMBOLISED IMMORTALITY BUT ALSO DOOM.

THE FORTINGHALL YEW IN PERTHSHIRE, SCOTLAND IS BETWEEN 2000 AND 3000 YEARS OLD. POSSIBLY THE OLDEST TREE IN BRITAIN.

OLIVE TREE.
OLEA EUROPAEA
FAM. OLEACEAE

A SMALL EVERGREEN NATIVE TO THE MEDITERRANEAN, ASIA AND NORTH AFRICA.

SEEDS CAN BE SOWN IN MILD SPRING WEATHER, BUT IT'S EASIER TO GROW OLIVE TREES FROM GRAFTING.

SHOULD BE PLANTED IN A SUNNY AREA WITH WELL-DRAINED SOIL.

ALTHOUGH IT ONLY BEARS FRUIT IN WARMER CLIMATES, IT IS HARDY ENOUGH TO STAND UP TO COOLER TEMPERATURES.

OLIVES AND OLIVE OIL HAVE SYMBOLIC REFERENCES OF PEACE, WISDOM, FERTILITY AND PURITY IN CONTEMPORARY AND ANCIENT CULTURES AROUND THE WORLD.

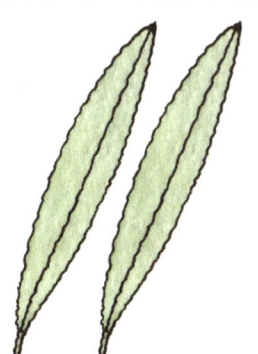

SHORT AND SQUAT WITH A TWISTED, GNARLY TRUNK.

SILVERY-GREEN POINTED LEAVES.
SLOW GROWING, SO DOESN'T NEED MUCH PRUNING.

FOSSILS OF OLIVE ANCESTORS DATE TO 30 MILLION YEARS AGO, WITH CULTIVATED OLIVES GROWN COMMERCIALLY FOR 6000 YEARS.

STONE PINE.

PINUS PINEA
FAM: PINACEAE

A MEDITERRANEAN PINE THAT IS CULTIVATED FOR ITS PINE NUTS.

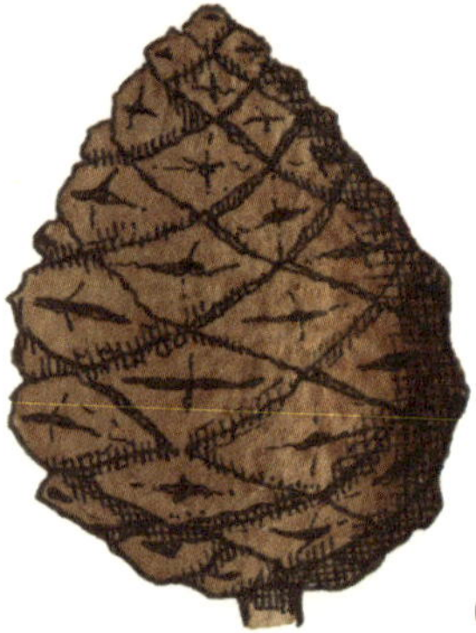

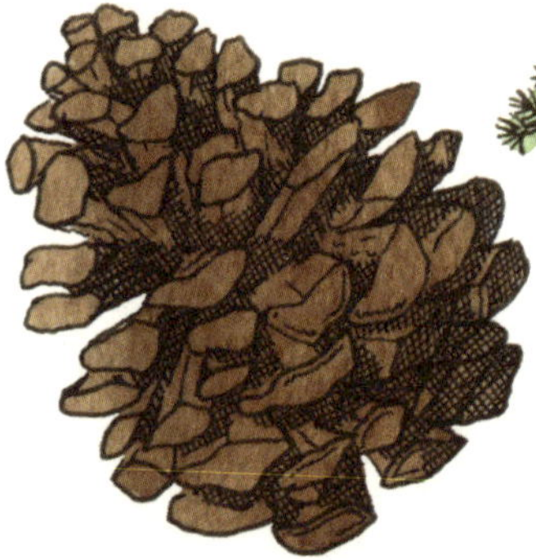

CONES ONLY START GROWING WHEN THE TREE IS AROUND 15 YEARS OLD.

THEY TAKE AROUND 36 MONTHS TO MATURE - LONGER THAN MOST CONES.

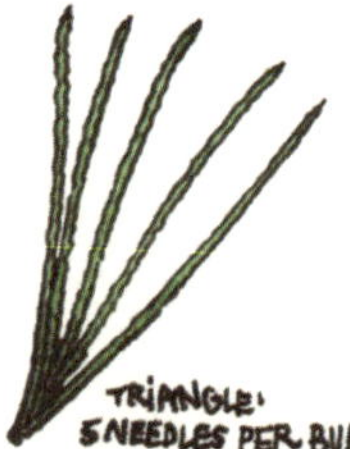

TRIANGLE:
5 NEEDLES PER BUNDLE.
ON THE SWISS STONE PINE.

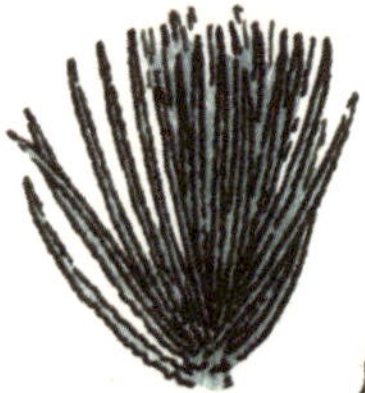

SILVERCREST.

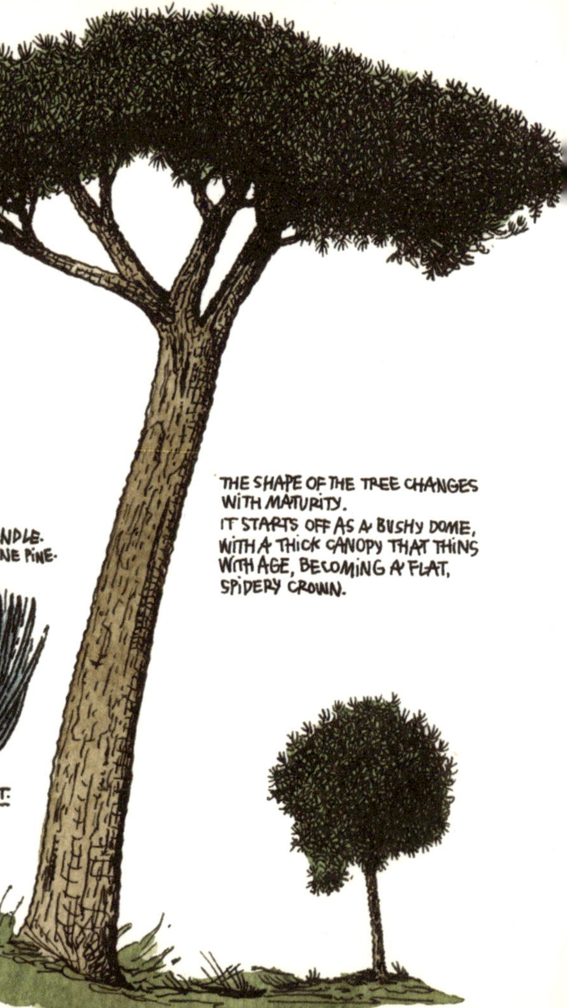

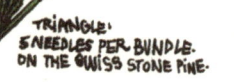

THE SHAPE OF THE TREE CHANGES WITH MATURITY.
IT STARTS OFF AS A BUSHY DOME, WITH A THICK CANOPY THAT THINS WITH AGE, BECOMING A FLAT, SPIDERY CROWN.

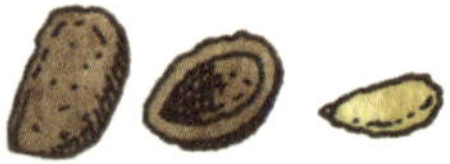

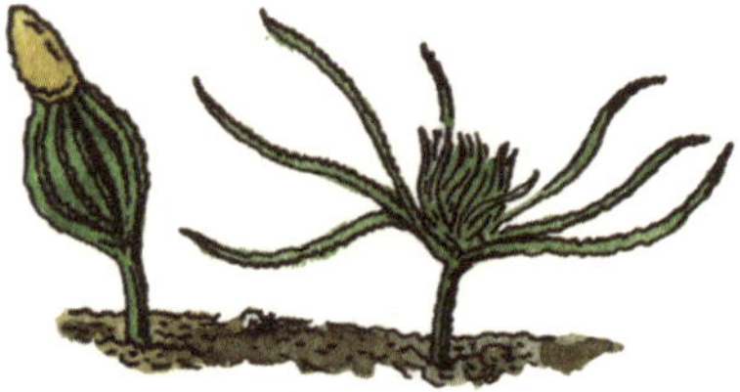

JUVENILE LEAVES GROW IN THICK BUNCHES OF SHORT, SOFT, SINGLE NEEDLES.

HAWTHORN.
CRATAEGUS MONOGYNA
FAM. ROSACEAE

SUMMER

AUTUMN

FRAGRANT WHITE OR PINK FLOWERS TURN INTO DEEP RED FRUIT CALLED "HAWS", WHICH MEANS "HEDGE" IN OLD ENGLISH.

HAWS ARE EDIBLE, BUT ARE BEST COOKED INTO JAM.

LEAVES VARY IN SHAPE BUT GROW IN SERRATED LOBES.

BROWN-GREY BARK COVERED IN SHARP THORNS.

YOUNG LEAVES CAN BE QUITE TASTY IN SALAD.

IT GROWS DENSELY AND CAN BE GROWN AS A BUSH OR A SMALL TREE. (GROWING TO AROUND 7 M HIGH.)

TRUE LEAF

PRIMARY LEAVES

HAWTHORNS ARE AN IMPORTANT PART OF TRADITIONAL ENGLISH ECOSYSTEMS, PROVIDING FOOD AND HABITATS FOR MANY BUTTERFLIES AND BIRDS. THEY ALSO HAVE AN AGE-OLD ASSOCIATION WITH FAIRIES.

BEST GROWN FROM GRAFTING, AS SEEDS CAN TAKE TWO YEARS TO GERMINATE.

I TRY TO PLANT MY TREES DIRECTLY INTO THE GROUND WHENEVER I CAN, BUT WITH A SMALL GARDEN, THIS ISN'T ALWAYS POSSIBLE, AND I HAVE A BROAD CIRCULATION OF TERRACOTTA POTS AT ALL TIMES.

STAGNANT WATER IS THE ENEMY OF TREES. POTS MUST HAVE HOLES TO DRAIN PROPERLY.

PUT A MESH SCREEN AT THE BASE OF YOUR POTS TO ALLOW A GOOD DRAIN BUT RETAIN THE SOIL.

SEEDLINGS SHOULD BE REPOTTED EVERY YEAR FOR THE FIRST THREE YEARS. A CHANGE OF SOIL, REPLENISHES THE TREES NUTRIENTS, AND REPOTTING ALSO ALLOWS YOU TO CHECK THE HEALTH OF THE ROOTS.

FAST GROWERS NEED A BIG POT FROM THE OUTSET, WHILST SLOW GROWERS PREFER SMALLER POTS, SO THEIR ROOTS DON'T GET TOO MOIST.

OAKS.
QUERCUS
FAM: FAGACEAE

King of the forest, the English Oak is probably the most beloved tree in Britain.

Acorns are delightful things. It's impossible not to love them.

To plant an acorn, choose one that's a little bit green as it is less likely to have insect damage.

Plant it head down in the soil. They almost always sprout.

Hardy, slow growing tree.

OAK IS A BIG FAMILY WITH VARIATIONS ALL OVER THE WORLD.

- WHITE OAK
- NORTHERN PIN
- RED.
- BUR
- BLACK
- SWAMP WHITE

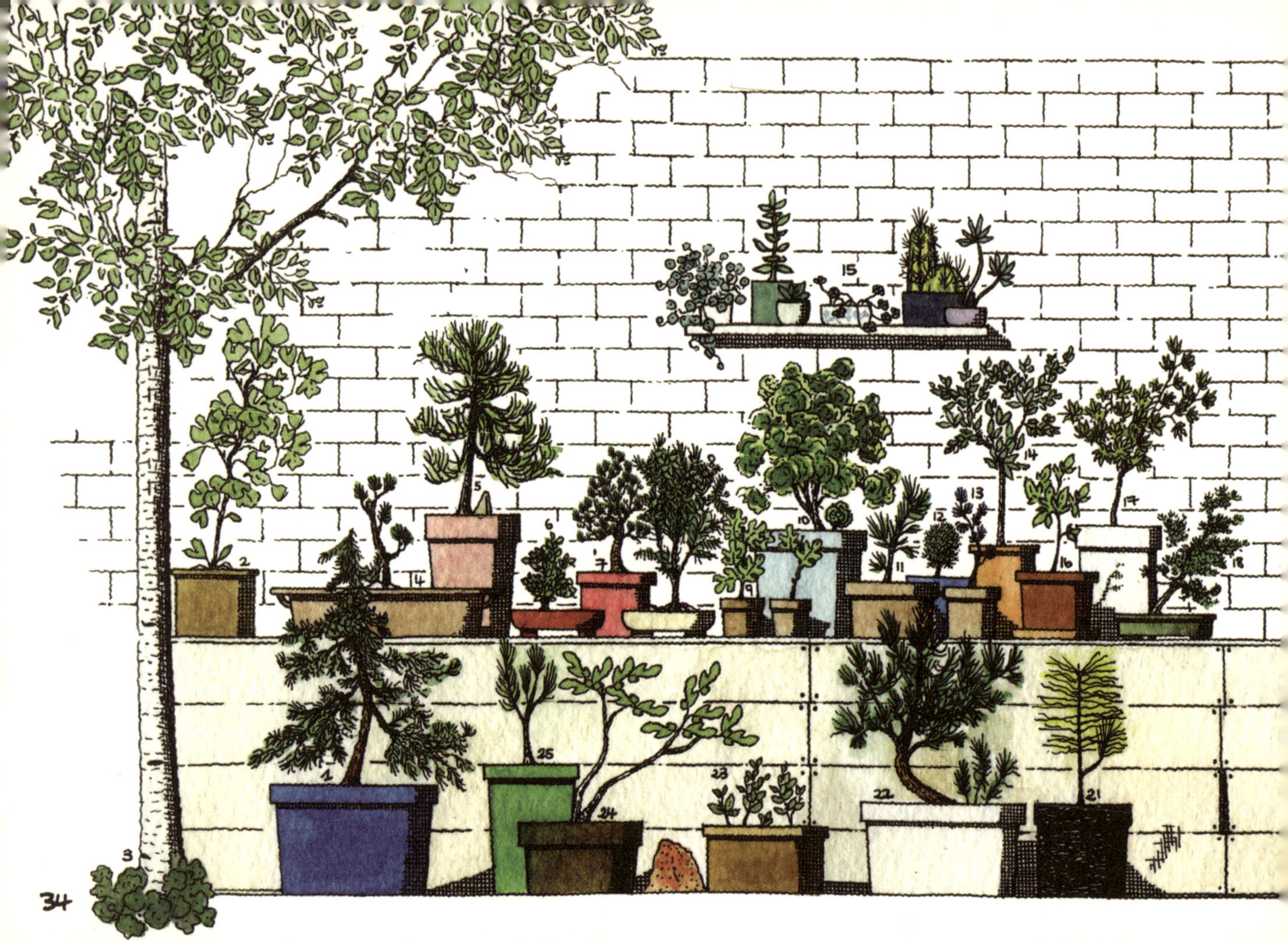
2
14
5
6
7
8
9
10
11
12
13
14
15
16
17
18
1
25
24
23
22
21
3

MY BENCH IN SUMMER.

THE ADRENALINE OF SPRING HAS STARTED TO SLOW.
IT'S TIME TO SIT BACK AND ENJOY THE FRUITS OF MY LABOURS
(AND SOMETIMES THE FRUITS OF THE TREES).

THE TREES MIGHT NEED AN OCCASIONAL WATERING,
BUT THE ONES IN THE GROUND SHOULD BE ABLE TO
WITHSTAND A BIT OF HEAT, SO FOR THE MOST PART,
I PUT MY FEET UP AND ENJOY THE VIEW.

1. COASTAL REDWOOD
2. GINKGO
3. SILVER BIRCH
4. JAPANESE WHITE PINE
5. GIANT SEQUOIA
6. COTONEASTER CORAL BEAUTY
7. LARCH
8. YEW
9. OAK
10. HINOKI CYPRESS
11. SCOTS PINE
12. PINUS STROBUS
13. ATLAS CEDAR
14. OLIVE TREE
15. SUCCULENTS
16. TRIDENT MAPLE
17. MOUNTAIN MAPLE
18. SAN JOSE JUNIPER
19. COLORADO BLUE SPRUCE
20. PRUNUS DOMESTICA
21. JAPANESE RED PINE
22. JAPANESE BLACK PINE
23. BOXWOOD
24. FIGTREE
25. STONE PINE

HINOKI CYPRESS.

CHAMAECYPARIS OPTUSA
FAM: CUPRESSACEAE

This Japanese evergreen is one of my top three favourite trees.

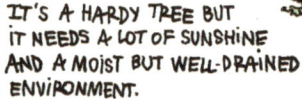

Leaves are graceful and fan-like with rounded tips.

It's a hardy tree but it needs a lot of sunshine and a moist but well-drained environment.

Its wood is pinkish, lemon-scented and rot resistant.

A slow-growing evergreen with reddish brown bark.

Mine is 70 cm and 10 years old.

There are different varieties — some reach 35 m, and others are dwarf evergreens that are more shrub-like.

The fragrant wood is also used as incense.

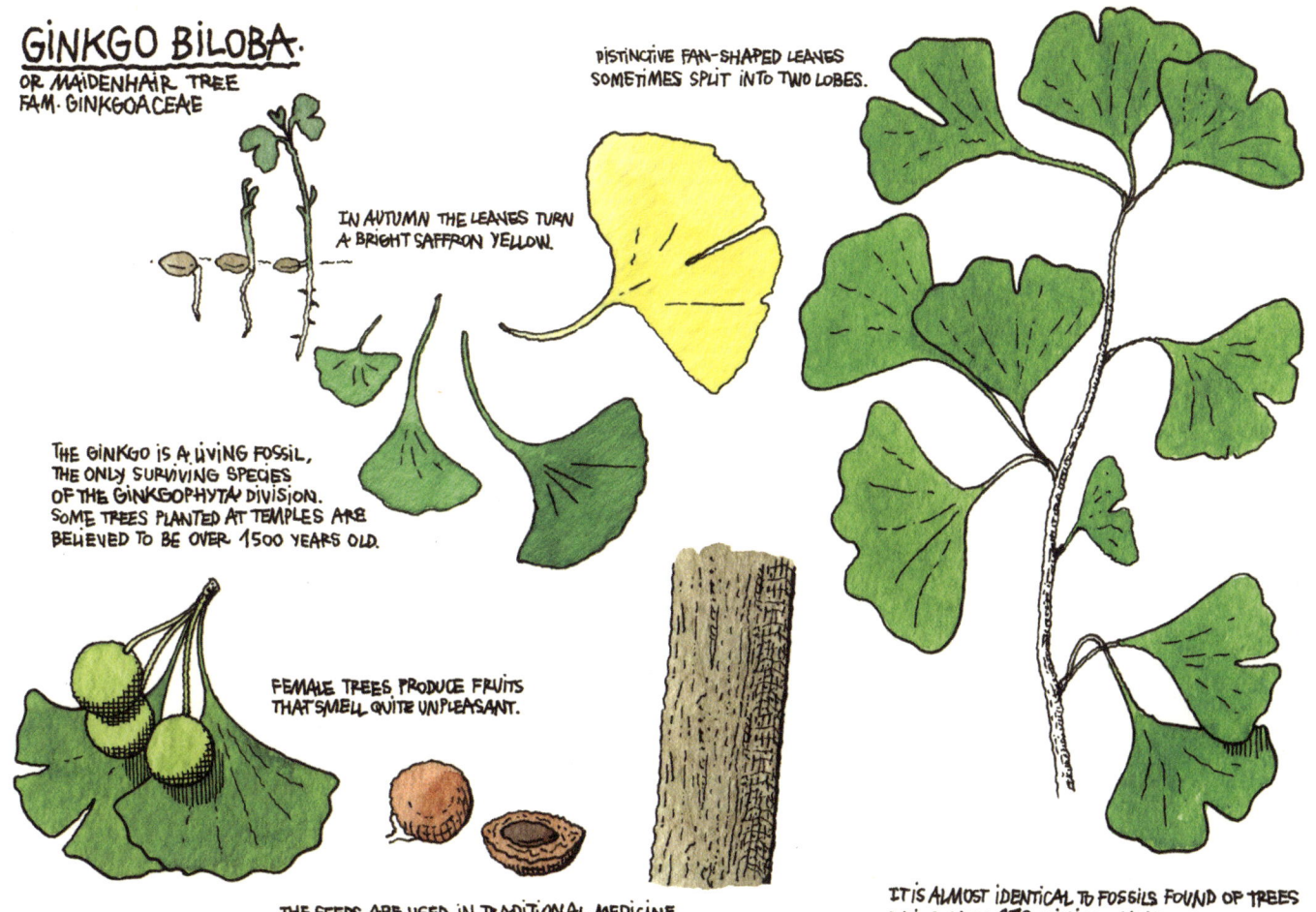

GINKGO BILOBA.
OR MAIDENHAIR TREE
FAM. GINKGOACEAE

Distinctive fan-shaped leaves sometimes split into two lobes.

In autumn the leaves turn a bright saffron yellow.

The Ginkgo is a living fossil, the only surviving species of the Ginkgophyta division. Some trees planted at temples are believed to be over 1500 years old.

Female trees produce fruits that smell quite unpleasant.

The seeds are used in traditional medicine and in Chinese and Japanese cooking.

It is almost identical to fossils found of trees dating back 270 million years.

37

PRUNUS DOMESTICA.
MARJORIE SEEDLING
FAM: ROSACEAE

A SMALL, SLIGHTLY THORNY DECIDUOUS TREE THAT IS THE MOST COMMONLY GROWN PLUM TREE IN EUROPE.

IN AUTUMN THEY TURN A DEEP RED.

THE LEAVES ARE OVAL-SHAPED, AROUND 10 CM LONG WITH WAVY EDGES.

IT LIKES MOIST, WELL-DRAINED, ACIDIC SOIL, AND IT NEEDS TO BE PLANTED IN A SHELTERED SPOT TO PROTECT ITS FLOWERS.

MY TREE GROWS SWEET DESSERT PLUMS THAT ARE OVAL IN SHAPE, RIPENING IN LATE SEPTEMBER. I EAT THEM OFF THE TREE OR COLLECT THEM TO MAKE JAM BUT THEY CAN ALSO BE USED TO MAKE A TYPE OF CIDER CALLED PLUM JERKUM.

IN SPRING, BEAUTIFUL WHITE FLOWERS GROW IN CLUSTERS OF TWO OR THREE.

LARCH.
Larix kaempferi
Fam. Pinaceae

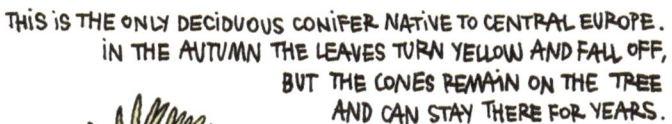

Ovoid cones.

This is the only deciduous conifer native to Central Europe. In the autumn the leaves turn yellow and fall off, but the cones remain on the tree and can stay there for years.

In English folklore, larch wood was said to protect against evil spirits.

Young trees are fast growing.

Soft, needle like leaves are a light green colour, 2-4 cm long, growing in tufts on the twigs.

COTONEASTER HORIZONTALIS.

AKA· WALL SPRAY. ROCK SPRAY
FAM· ROSACEAE

IT WAS ORIGINALLY NATIVE TO WESTERN CHINA BUT IT TAKES WELL-DRAINED SOIL OF ANY CLIMATE.

EASY AND FAST GROWER.

2/3 MM

SPRING SUMMER AUTUMN

BERRIES. 5 MM

"ROTHSCHILDIANUS"

"WATERERI PINK CHAMPAGNE"

THE LEAVES TAKE A FLAT, SYMMETRICAL HERRINGBONE PATTERN.

IT FLOWERS IN EARLY SUMMER WITH WHITE BLOSSOMS, ATTRACTING BEES AND BUTTERFLIES.

IN AUTUMN, DEEP RED FRUITS EMERGE ALL ALONG ITS BRANCHES.

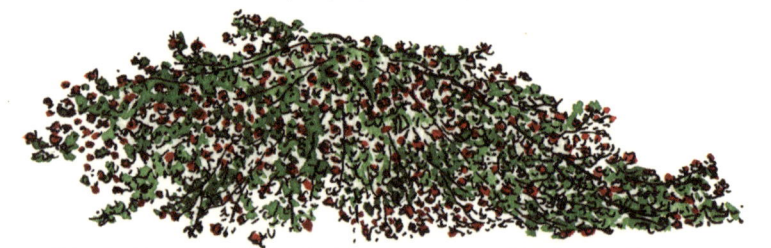

COTONEASTER FRANCHETII

WILLOW-LEAF COTONEASTER

COTONEASTER GLAUCOUS.

THE COTONEASTER IS A VERY COMMON, FAST-GROWING, DECIDUOUS TREE.

PINUS STROBUS
SEA URCHIN
FAM. PINACEAE

A WHITE PINE TREE NATIVE TO THE EAST COAST OF NORTH AMERICA. IT HAS LONG, BLUISH-GREEN NEEDLES THAT GROW UP TO 15 CM LONG IN GROUPS OF FIVE.

CONES ARE CYLINDRICAL AND VERY RESINOUS.

THE NEEDLES CAN BE MADE INTO HERBAL TEA. THEY ARE VERY RICH IN VITAMIN C — FIVE TIMES AS RICH AS LEMONS.

IT GROWS VERY FAST WHEN IT'S MATURE, BUT MINE ONLY GROWS AROUND ONE OR TWO INCHES A YEAR.

TINY PEBBLE

IT GROWS IN A GLOBE-SHAPE, WHICH IS WHY IT'S SOMETIMES CALLED A SEA URCHIN TREE.

IT LIKES A WELL-DRAINED SOIL AND FULL SUN.

MY TREE IS 5 YEARS OLD.

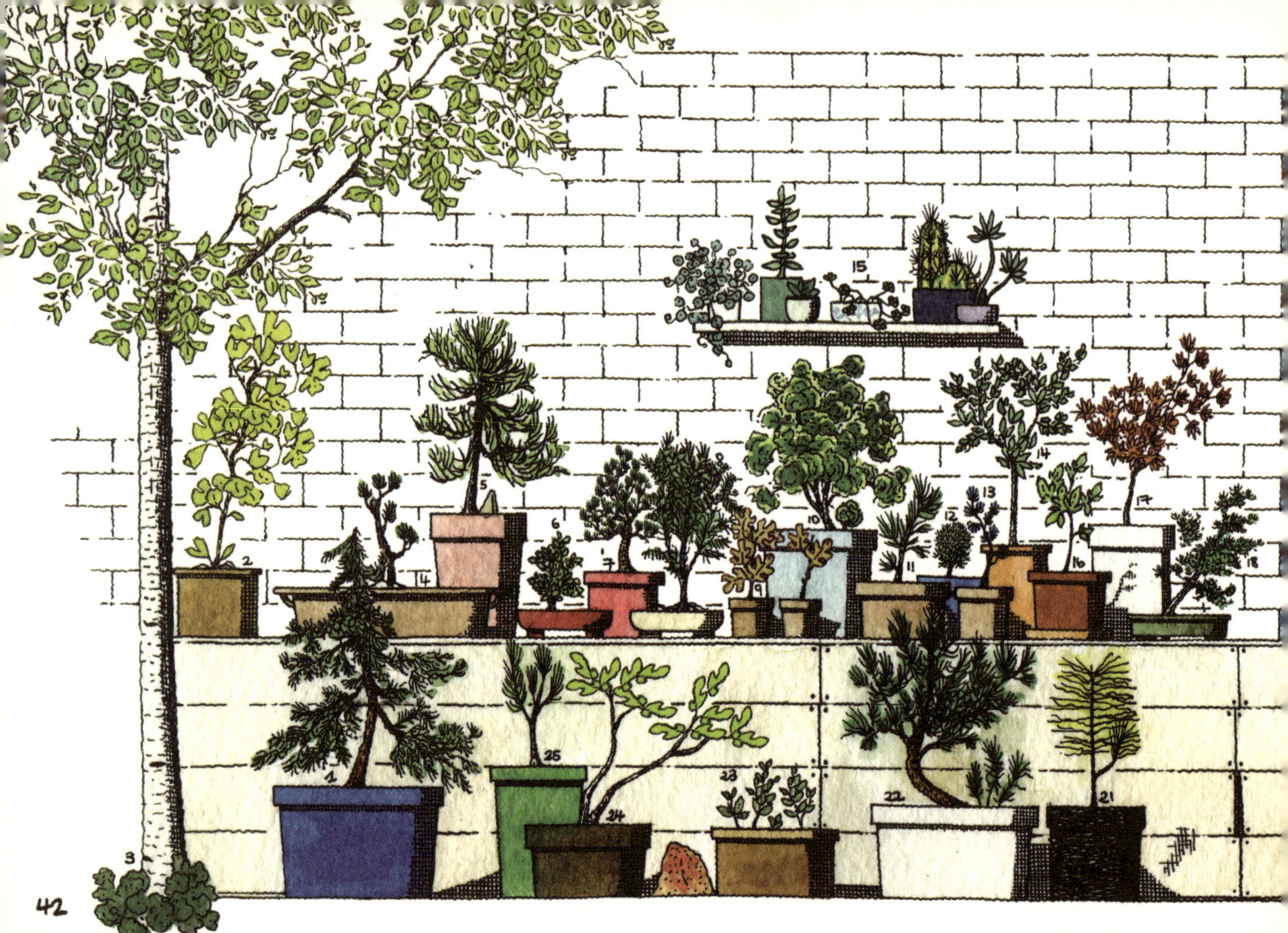
1
2
3
4
5
6
7
8
9
10
11
12
13
14
15
16
17
18
21
22
23
24
25

MY BENCH IN AUTUMN.

I try to have plenty of specimens with good foliage, so when October rolls around, my bench becomes a gradient of hues from green to yellow, orange and red. Growth slows as the trees prepare for winter.

Autumn is also when I go to the woods, collecting seeds and cones, drying them out and storing them until spring when I can start all over again.

1. Coastal Redwood
2. Ginkgo
3. Silver Birch
4. Japanese White Pine
5. Giant Sequoia
6. Cotoneaster Coral Beauty
7. Larch
8. Yew
9. Oak
10. Hinoki Cypress
11. Scots Pine
12. Pinus Strobus
13. Atlas Cedar
14. Olive Tree
15. Succulents
16. Trident Maple
17. Mountain Maple
18. San Jose Juniper
19. Colorado Blue Spruce
20. Prunus Domestica
21. Japanese Red Pine
22. Japanese Black Pine
23. Boxwood
24. Figtree
25. Stone Pine

PEOPLE HAVE ASKED ME WHAT I PLAN TO DO WITH MY TREES
WHEN I MOVE HOUSE, OR WHEN THEY GET TOO BIG.
THE HONEST TRUTH IS THAT I HAVEN'T WORKED IT OUT YET.
I WOULD LOVE TO GIVE THE RARER SPECIMENS TO SOME KIND
OF CONSERVATION SOCIETY, SOME TO FRIENDS WHO HAVE SPACE,
AND MAYBE ONE DAY CREATE MY VERY OWN ARBORETUM.
I WANT TO BELIEVE THAT THEY WILL THRIVE AND OUTLIVE ME.